CANALS AND INLAND WATERWAYS

Front Cover Picture:
Chelmer & Blackwater Navigation, Maldon 1906 (55547)

Above:
The Staircase Locks, Bingley c1900 (B98501)

FRANCIS FRITH AND HIS UNIQUE ARCHIVE

In 1860, Francis Frith, the Quaker son of a Chesterfield cooper, was 38 years old. He had already sold a massive grocery business that he had built up for a small fortune. Like Livingstone and Stanley, Frith was fired with a romantic Wanderlust, and the Victorian deep passion for travelling and exploring. Between 1857 and 1859 he made several pioneering photographic journeys to remote regions of the Nile that brought him considerable fame.

After his marriage in 1860, he confined his wanderings a little closer to home and began a series of photo trips around Britain. His aim was to make his pictures available to the greatest number of people possible - life was hard and drab for millions of Victorians, and Frith believed his 'view souvenirs' of seaside resorts, beauty spots and town and village scenes would help keep their rare days out alive in their memories. He was right: by 1890 he had created the largest photographic publishing company in the world!

As well as thousands of views of high streets around Britain, Frith's growing archive included beautiful scenes of leafy glades, dusty lanes, rocks and coastlines, and the boats and riversides, beloved of Victorian wanderers like Jerome K Jerome - whose 'Three Men in a Boat' had struck a strong chord with the public.

Life in the Frith family was never dull. The family went with him on many trips, and the highlights were recorded by his wife, Mary Ann, in her journal. In 1872 she tells of a relaxing three week expedition to Ilfracombe in North Devon. Whilst such trips may have been something of a holiday for his wife and children, Francis Frith found no time to put his feet up. He was up and down the coast photographing Barnstaple and Lynton, hiring carters to carry him out to remote locations, and boatsmen to row him round the bay to view and photograph spectacular cliff formations.

After Francis Frith died in 1898 his sons carried on the business for many years with great success, specialising in postcards and other prints. So impressive is the archive he started that **The Financial Times** called it '*a unique and priceless record of English life in the last century*'.

Canals and Inland Waterways

A Journey Through Frith's England

This edition published by
The Francis Frith Collection exclusively for
Selectabook Ltd., Roundway, Devizes,
Wiltshire SN10 2HR

Picture compilation and text by Terence Sackett

First Published in 1996

ISBN 1 85937 028 4

Printed in Italy by Imago Publishing

Reproductions of all the photographs in this book are available as framed or mounted prints from The Francis Frith Collection at the address below. Please quote the town, full title and negative number shown in brackets.

The Francis Frith Collection
The Old Rectory, Bimport, Shaftesbury, Dorset SP7 8AT
Tel: 01747 855669 Fax: 01747 855065

Contents

The South and South West	7 - 17
Up the River Thames	18 - 24
Around the Thames	25 - 32
Up the Rivers Severn and Avon	33 - 38
Towards the Midlands	39 - 50
The North Midlands	51 - 59
Around Merseyside	60 - 69
East Anglia and the Fens	70 - 85
The North and North East	86 - 99
The North West	100 - 111
Index	112

INTRODUCTION

The rivers of England have been used for carrying freight since medieval times. Many have been systematically improved down the centuries, with banks being reinforced, shallows dredged, and weirs bypassed with locks.

During the early years of the Industrial Revolution, factory owners and industrialists felt a strong need for new waterways that would link regional manufacturing centres with the major cities and ports. The Duke of Bridgewater built the first canal, linking his mines at Worsley with the expanding city of Manchester. There soon followed a huge network of canals straddling the country, joining north with south and east with west. Many made important connections with the older river navigations. They were remarkable feats of engineering, with pioneering giants like Telford and Brindley forging smooth waterways through seemingly impossible terrain.

Yet the canals enjoyed only a short period of success. The railways followed quickly in their wake, poaching much of their freight business. By the early 1900s the canals had declined in importance, some fallen into dereliction. Many we see today have taken on a new role as lesiure waterways for pleasure boats, although others, such as the Manchester Ship Canal, still play a major role in the transportation of freight.

The Victorians had a deep love of messing around in boats and this is reflected in the many pictures of the Thames and other river navigations, busy at weekends and in the summer months with steam launches, skiffs and punts. The Norfolk Broads are now almost entirely used for leisure but link up with rivers that were once vital regional commercial waterways. The Lake District, beloved of the Victorian tripper, is depicted, too, Windermere being the greatest of our inland lakes.

A Journey Through England

In this selection of photographs from the Frith archive, we take a nostalgic journey along the inland waterways of England.

The book explains where each canal or waterway shown begins and ends, and where they link together to form strategic regional networks. We begin in the southern counties, moving westwards from Kent through to Cornwall, then travel gradually northwards via Bristol and the River Thames. The canals and waterways that link up with the Thames around London and the Home Counties are grouped together. There follows a journey up the Severn and Avon rivers. In the Midlands the canals are at their most numerous, thickly knotted around Birmingham. The large number of connections and junctions underline how vital the network was to the success of the Industrial Revolution. North of Birmingham they stretch out towards Manchester and the Mersey. Then we explore the waterways of East Anglia, and finally those of the north, north east and north west, including the Lake District.

Please note: all locations, titles and dates for photographs in this book have been taken from the Frith & Co ledgers.

Above: The Medway Navigation at Aylesford 1898 (41549)

THE SOUTH AND SOUTH WEST

Canals are scarce in the extreme southern counties of Britain. Throughout the Industrial Revolution, which was the main driving force of the great canal building era, the south stayed largely rural. Where produce had to travel long distances across country, it was largely shipped round the coast between Cornwall and London, then up one of the river navigations. Kent was served by the Medway, and Sussex by the Ouse, the Arun and the old Portsmouth & Arundel Canal. There was a dearth of inland waterways in Hampshire and Dorset. In Devon the Dart, the Exe and Salcombe rivers carried commercial traffic, but they are now largely for pleasure craft. Cornwall had its own tiny canal at Bude. Only at Bristol was there anything approaching a major waterway - the Avon, which via the Kennet & Avon Canal and the River Thames, connected the region to London.

Above: *The Medway winds its way between muddy banks to Aylesford, with its fine old 14th-century stone bridge. Shallow-draught sailing barges, such as those moored here, plied between the Medway ports and the estuary, carrying straw bales and agricultural produce.*

Above: The River Medway, Maidstone 1892 (31483)

THE MEDWAY NAVIGATION

From the Thames estuary at Sheerness via Maidstone to Tonbridge in Kent

The navigation on the River Medway was developed for barges carrying timber for shipbuilding from the forests of the Kentish Weald to the naval dockyards at Chatham. They also carried chalk from Kent quarries to Gravesend. The river loops a sinuous course through hopfields and orchards to Maidstone.

THE RIVER ROTHER

From Rye Harbour on the Sussex Coast to Bodiam

The roofs and church tower of Rye, the lovely old town set by the Romney Marshes, cluster on a low hill in the background. Below is a plethora of warehouses and a timber-boarded smock mill.

Above: The River Rother at Rye 1901 (47445)

Above: The River Ouse, Lewes c1900 (L40080)

THE RIVER OUSE

From Newhaven to Lewes, Sussex

Close to 10 miles long, this South Coast tidal waterway had already fallen into disrepair by the 1860s. There were locks above Lewes, which is shown here.

THE CHICHESTER CANAL

From Chichester Harbour to Casher Lock, Sussex

This tiny stretch, less than a mile long, is all that is left of the grandiose Portsmouth & Arundel Canal, which linked Ford on the River Arun with Chichester and Portsmouth Harbour. It opened in 1823, but soon faced local opposition, when residents complained that seawater was seeping from it into their wells and contaminating the drinking water. The company ignored the protests but failed to drum up trade, and the canal was derelict by the 1860s.

Above: The Canal, Chichester 1898 (42684)

THE EXETER SHIP CANAL

From the Exe estuary to the city of Exeter, Devon

Exeter's canal was built at the request of the city's Tudor merchants and traders, who were exasperated by the weirs on the River Exe that obstructed the free flow of water transport into the city. John Trew's pioneering canal was miniscule, just 3 feet deep and 16 feet wide. It boasted the first pound locks in Britain. In the 1820s, James Green widened the canal considerably, carving it out to a depth of 15 feet so that it could carry vessels of several hundred tons up to the city canal basin. Yet it never truly prospered after these costly improvements, the city's woollen export trade having declined. This approach to the city is picturesque, the canal winding its way between meadows and reed-fringed banks.

Above: Exeter from the Canal 1929 (82302)

Above: Exeter from the Canal 1896 (38033)

Above: Canal Lock, Exeter 1906 (53983)

Above: The Port, Exeter 1896 (38034)

THE SALCOMBE RIVER

From Salcombe to Kingsbridge, Devon

In the picture opposite, we see the steamer 'Totnes Castle' carrying trippers up the river to this attractive old market town. Kingsbridge had been an important port since medieval times, and a centre for the exporting of wool to the continent.

THE FOWEY RIVER

From Bodmin via Lostwithiel to Fowey, Cornwall

There could hardly be a greater contrast in mood between these two photographs. The top picture shows the Fowey beloved of weekend salts and retired admirals who sip gins on the verandahs of waterside houses in this timeless old town. A mile up river, great ships slide past the yachts to the industrial wharf. Here they load up with china clay brought down by rail from St Austell.

Above: The River at Fowey 1898 (41958)

Above: The Docks at Fowey 1908 (60901). *Opposite:* The Promenade, Kingsbridge 1920 (69824)

Above: The Falcon Hotel at Bude 1900 (45878)
Below: The Lock and Breakwater, Bude 1893 (31893)

THE BUDE CANAL

From Bude to Rodd's Bridge, Cornwall

The Bude Canal was built in 1823 for the passage of 5 ton tub-boats. It featured hydraulic inclined planes instead of locks for negotiating changes in level. The tub-boats, which had iron wheels, were hauled up a railed track. By the 1830s over 30 miles of canal had been constructed, transporting 50,000 tons of sea sand a year from the north Cornwall coast for use as fertilizer on inland farms. It was closed, except for the section at Bude, in 1891.

THE RIVER AVON

From the Kennet & Avon Canal, via Bath, to the Bristol Channel

This impressive 16 mile long navigation was created by John Hore in the 1720s to connect Bristol with Bath. Here we see the river snaking its way through the steep rocky flanks of the Avon gorge. The spectacular Clifton Suspension Bridge was built by Brunel in 1864. The harbour at Bristol, pictured overleaf, was once the busy hub of the city, and Bristol-based ships were to be seen in ports all over the world. Wines, tobaccos and timber were discharged at the dock. At Prince's Wharf, Brunel's pioneering steamship, 'The Great Western', was proudly launched. At one time the river was crowded with barges and wide-beam tankers, but the canal basin and harbour are now silent and all but deserted.

Above: Clifton Bridge 1887 (20167)

Above: The Harbour, Bristol c1950 (B212181) *Overleaf:* The Quay, Bristol 1887 (20133)

Above: Teddington Bridge 1899 (43050)
Opposite: Houseboats in Molesey Lock 1896 (38350)

UP THE RIVER THAMES

Today we think of the Thames as the home of regattas and boating holidays. It was for the Victorians, too - the languid pleasure of punting, rowing and messing about in boats was one of their favourite pastimes. Jerome K Jerome's book about a voyage between Kingston and Oxford is an idler's delight. But the Thames in the Victorian era was also bustling with commercial traffic. Sailing barges plied between the port of London and the towns of the Thames Valley, and transhipped their cargoes to other barges travelling yet further west along the Kennet & Avon Canal, and so on to Bath and Bristol. The Thames was also linked with the Basingstoke Canal, and with the River Wey navigation that once connected Surrey with the Sussex coast. Barges from the Grand Union Canal entered the Thames with goods from the Midlands. Freight carrying on the Thames only declined with the huge success of the Great Western Railway, which connected London with Bristol in less than three hours.

Above: *Thames sailing barges moor under the bridge at Teddington. In the foreground are a trio of pleasure boats with awnings.*

Above: Maidenhead, Boulters Lock 1925 (77624)

THE RIVER THAMES

Molesey, Surrey and Maidenhead, Berkshire

The picture on the previous page shows a party on a steam launch at Molesey Lock. Luncheon has been consumed and the two housemaids are enjoying a well-earned rest. And they needed it - they would have been up since dawn, preparing joints of cold roast beef, fowls, parcels of duck, ham, veal pie and collared calf's head, all followed by stewed fruit, cabinet pudding and plum cake. During Ascot week the Thames was thronged with skiffs and steam launches. Jerome K Jerome, in 'Three Men in a Boat', records how you could barely see any water at all on a summer's afternoon, just like the bustling scene below. The river was a riot of colour, a brilliant tangle of bright blazers, caps and saucy hats.

Above: East Molesey, Lock, 'Coming Over the Rollers' 1896 (38346)

Above: Henley On Thames Regatta, 1890 (27200)

THE RIVER THAMES

Henley, Oxfordshire and Sonning, Berkshire

The world-famous Henley Regatta was first contested in 1839. Oarsmen raced up river from Temple Island to below the town bridge. It was much more than just a race, and quickly developed into one of the most prestigious events in the social calendar, where the upper classes could dress up, eat, drink and be merry, and cheer themselves hoarse. The view of Sonning, just a few miles upstream, could not depict a greater contrast. This tranquil scene shows the old brick, many-arched bridge, with Sonning's picturesque jumble of cottages in the background. The punt on the right has the waterway all to itself.

Above: The Bridge and River, Sonning 1890 (27153)

THE RIVER THAMES

Caversham and Reading, Berkshire

The navigability of the River Thames has been under continual improvement since the 18th century. Eight timber pound locks were built on the stretch between Reading and Maidenhead, permitting the passage of 150 ton barges. Many hauled sea coal to the towns and villages of the Thames Valley. Reading grew rapidly in the Victorian era, with companies such as Huntley & Palmer establishing factories in the town. Yet the river still had its quiet stretches, offering peace and respite from the harsh world of work. The river banks at Reading and Caversham are fringed with boatyards renting out small craft. The Kennet & Avon Canal begins its long trek across Wiltshire here at Reading, from the inauspicious setting of the gas works.

Top: Caversham from Bridge 1890 (27099). *Centre:* Caversham Lock, Reading 1912 (64647)
Above: Reading 1912 (64648)

Above: The Lock, Mapledurham 1890 (27089)
Below: The Lock, Goring 1896 (38312)

THE RIVER THAMES

Mapledurham and Goring, Oxfordshire

Close by Pangbourne and sheltered by wooded slopes, Mapledurham is the quintessential Thames-side village. It has the last working watermill on the river. The writer Robert Gibbings records that 450 housemartins nested under the arches of the bridge. The sight of them swooping low over the water after flies, and cutting across the bows of the boats, must have been breathtaking. At Goring there is a lock, a weir and a bridge, and the river dips through a deep, tree-lined gorge.

THE RIVER THAMES

Abingdon, Iffley and Streatley, Oxfordshire

In the 17th century there was a separate navigation channel at Abingdon known as Swift Ditch, which bypassed the town. The present day route under the town bridge was opened in the 1790s. Beyond the lock shown here, the river flows through a magnificent stretch of broad parkland at Nuneham. The mill at Iffley, depicted in the romantic and atmospheric old view shown here, was destroyed by fire in 1907. Like so many of the small Thames-side watermills, it found itself unable to compete with the modern industrial mills that were springing up across the country. Streatley was the province of anglers, many of whom stayed at the lovely old riverside inn, The Swan Hotel, pictured here. The river abounded in pike, roach, gudgeon and eels. Jerome K Jerome records how jack and perch would come and 'stand half out of the water with their mouths open' begging for biscuits.

Top: The Lock, Abingdon 1890 (26990). *Centre:* The Mill, Lock and Bridge, Iffley 1890 (26959)
Above: The Swan Hotel, Streatley 1899 (42994)

Above: The Lock, Hertford, River Lee 1929 (81783)

AROUND THE THAMES

The River Thames links up with several waterways that carried goods shipped to the port of London out into the counties of the Thames Valley and beyond. In London itself, the River Lee served the northern fringes as far as the town of Hertford. The Basingstoke Canal carried mainly agricultural produce for the capital's fast-growing population. The Wey Navigation linked the city with the market towns of Surrey. The major canal of the region is the Kennet & Avon, which forged a vital course west from the Thames at Reading all the way through to Bath, where it spilled into the Avon and joined London with the Bristol Channel. The rivers of the region were not all commercial, however: at Oxford, the Cherwell was the perfect setting for punting away the long summer afternoons.

Above: *Since medieval times, the Lee has been a busy trade route for craft plying between London and its northern fringes. Before the Victorian urbanisation of London's hinterland, much of the countryside bordering the Lee would have been as picturesque as this scene of the lock at Hertford.*

Above: Odiham, Basingstoke Canal 1906 (55854)

Above: Frimley Green, Basingstoke Canal 1927 (79630)

THE BASINGSTOKE CANAL

From the Wey at Byfleet, Surrey to Greywell, Hampshire

This canal was constructed in 1796 and runs for nearly forty miles through northern Hampshire. It was never a financial success because of its strictly rural course. The owners had hoped they could gain business carrying goods bound for the western counties, but the success of the Kennet & Avon Canal put paid to their hopes. In the early 1800s the Basingstoke company was charging 6s 2d for moving a load of timber 27 miles - canal tolls were often only a third of those charged by road carriers - but even this did not halt the canal's decline. Costs rose dramatically in the Victorian era and the company was forced into liquidation. The Basingstoke eventually fell into disrepair and dereliction. The spectacular 1,200 yard long tunnel at Greywell, near Odiham, collapsed in the 1930s.

Above: Send, Wey Navigation 1909 (61923)

Above: Send, Wey Navigation 1909 (61924)

Above: Boating on the River Wey, Godalming 1908 (59957)
Below: Boat houses, Guildford, River Wey 1911 (63171)

THE WEY NAVIGATION

From the Thames at Weybridge via Guildford to Godalming, Surrey

The Wey Navigation is a 17th-century engineering tour de force. Sir Richard Weston not only built 12 bridges along its length, but his 10 pound locks and weirs overcome an overall fall of 86 feet. There is still a rare partly turf-sided lock at New Haw. The Worsfold Gate Lock at Send, shown on the previous page, features paddle gear, also now very rare, but which could once be seen in many places on the navigation. Boats ferried a wide range of goods, including grain and bricks.

Above: Dunn Mill, Hungerford, Kennet and Avon Canal c1955 (H134018)

THE KENNET AND AVON CANAL

From the Thames at Reading to Hanham on the Bristol Avon

Fifty-seven miles long, this spectacular cross-country canal connects the River Thames with the Bristol Channel. It opened in 1810. It winds a sinuous course through some of the most beautiful countryside in the south. 79 locks carry craft to a summit of 474 feet at Savernake. At Hungerford, pictured here, there is a wharf and warehouse and an old red-brick stone bridge carrying the town's traffic. Just a little further along from Hungerford is the 500-yard long Bruce Tunnel. The Canal showed early promise for shareholders, but the success of freight hauling on the Great Western Railway put paid to further expansion - goods reached London from Bristol in three hours. The Kennet and Avon was tragically unable to compete.

Above: Hungerford, Kennet and Avon Canal 1903 (49389)

Above: Devizes, Kennet and Avon Canal 1898 (42319)

Above: The Caen Lock Flight, Devizes, Kennet and Avon Canal 1898 (42320)

THE KENNET AND AVON CANAL

From the Thames at Reading to Hanham on the Bristol Avon

One of the grandest and most daunting sights on the Kennet and Avon is the extraordinary flight of 29 locks at Caen Hill, Devizes. The pattern created by their many extending balance beams has been compared with the backbone of a huge reptile. Though each lock has a side-pond to help store some of the water, each time the flight is operated 11 million gallons disappear downhill! Lining the canal at the pretty village of Bathampton are simple terraces, but travellers are soon rewarded with some superb views over the roofs of the city. The canal approaches the city of Bath in style. It drops rapidly towards Bath down the Widcombe flight of six locks, and joins the River Avon in the very heart of the city. Pulteney Bridge, carrying its bijou shops overhead, is a picture of sophisticated Classical architecture, and provides a grand finale to the Kennet & Avon's spectacular progress across southern Britain.

Top: Bridge and Weir, Bath 1914 (67451). *Centre:* On the Canal at Bath 1895 (35759)
Above: George Inn, Bathampton, Kennet and Avon Canal 1907 (57749)

THE RIVER CHERWELL

Through Oxfordshire to the Oxford Canal

The River Cherwell leads us into an enchanted world of idleness and pleasure, remote from the commercial bustle of the canals. It is continually obstructed by weirs as it crosses rural Oxfordshire, and has never been a serious commercial proposition. In the top picture of Oxford shown here, students enjoy the leafy silence of the Cherwell's backwaters, punting away the lazy summer afternoon. The ladies shelter from the sun beneath great parasols. Yet the rivers of Oxford were not always the place to go to enjoy a little peace and quiet - in the lower picture the waters are almost heaving with punts.

Above: On the River Cherwell, Oxford 1906 (53704).

Above: On the River Cherwell, Oxford 1922 (72053)

Above: The Lydney Canal, Forest of Dean c1960 (L200036)

UP THE RIVER SEVERN AND THE RIVER AVON

The great river of the west is the Severn. Navigable from Stourport, it has important connections with the Midland network of canals, including the Staffordshire & Worcestershire and the Worcester & Birmingham. A river infamous for its high tides and the formidable Bore, it flows out into the Bristol Channel. There are important docks at Gloucester. The Severn was once busy with barges that plied as far up river as Welshpool. The Warwickshire Avon can be considered as two separate waterways: the lower section streams into the Severn at Tewkesbury, and is now navigable only as far as Evesham; the Upper section became impassable to commercial traffic in the 1870s, and is now the province of skiffs and punts, that glide along the still waters through Shakespeare's Stratford.

Above: *The miniscule Lydney Canal is no more than a mile in length, with just a single lock. Pictured here are barges carrying timber from Avonmouth Docks to the industrial yard on the left. The trade declined in the 1970s.*

NEW RED LION INN

Above: The Docks, Gloucester 1923 (73689) *Opposite:* Chalford, Stroudwater Canal 1910 (62711)

THE STROUDWATER CANAL

Between Saul Junction and the River Severn, Gloucestershire

The charming scene opposite shows children playing alongside the Stroudwater Canal at Chalford. It was specially built to accommodate the elegant sailing barges called Severn trows. The canal closed in 1954.

THE RIVER SEVERN

From Stourport, Worcestershire to Gloucester

The high banks along many stretches of this great river confirm its habit of flooding. The Severn is no longer a major route for commercial traffic but does link up with some significant Midland canals. At Gloucester, boats and barges, carrying mainly timber and grain, could pass into the basin by way of a lock. In the picture of the docks on this page, neat rows of empty steel barges are lined up alongside the quay at Wait James & Company's warehouse.

Above: Gloucester from the River Severn 1923 (73673)

THE RIVER SEVERN

From Stourport, Worcestershire to Gloucester

At Holt Fleet, in the top picture on this page, an elegant iron bridge spans the River Severn. A steam launch is carrying a party of trippers past the Holt Fleet Hotel. It is a regular venue for boats - note the three landing stages. In the distance, on the right, is the lock.

The 14th-century tower of Worcester Cathedral provides a magnificent backdrop for the river traveller. As the boat glides along between willow-fringed water meadows, there are tantalising glimpses of the delights of this historic city.

In the 1800s, barges were able to travel up the Severn as far as Welshpool, several miles beyond Shrewsbury. Now Stourport is the practical limit of navigation.

The Severn at Shrewsbury is the haunt of pleasure-craft. Here the ferryman is carrying guests from the Boat House Inn across the river.

Top: Holt Fleet, River Severn 1907 (59103). *Centre:* Worcester Cathedral and River Severn 1923 (73749)
Above: Boat House Inn, Shrewsbury, River Severn 1911 (63218)

Above: From the Bridge over the River Severn, Stourport 1931 (84626)

THE RIVER AVON

From the Severn at Tewkesbury to Alveston, Warwickshire, plus a junction with the Southern Stratford Canal

There are 17 locks on this very beautiful river, which penetrates to the very heart of England at Shakespeare's Stratford. In this tranquil scene at Evesham, shown on the right, a girl in a pinafore dress is hauling at a rope on the Hampton Ferry, carrying her younger brother across the river. Since the early 1700s the Avon has been divided into two halves at Evesham - the Upper and Lower - owned and managed separately. The Upper section has been impassable by commercial boats for over a century. An example of the improvement work carried out on the Lower section of the waterway below Evesham is plain to see in the photograph of Mythe Bridge, between Tewkesbury and Twyning, overleaf. A rough load of timber has been stacked on the banks awaiting collection.

Above: Hampton Ferry over the River Avon, Evesham 1895 (36969)

Above: Mythe Bridge over the River Avon, Tewkesbury 1891 (29360)

Above: The River Avon at Stratford 1922 (72393)

Above: Banbury, The Oxford Canal 1921 (70593)

TOWARDS THE MIDLANDS

Two great canals forge a route into the heart of England from the south. The Grand Union Canal is an amalgamation of several older waterways. From the Thames at Brentford, Middlesex, it journeys north towards Birmingham linking many important industrial and commercial centres. There are strategic branch canals on the way, including those at Aylesbury and Leicester. The Oxford Canal has always been a poor neighbour of the Grand Union. Yet it creates a vital long-distance link with the rest of the Midlands network at Napton and Braunston, and with the Coventry Canal. Together with the Staffordshire & Worcestershire, it is part of the Grand Cross system linking the Thames, Severn, Trent and Mersey. The Birmingham Canal Navigations are a complex knot of small waterways serving Birmingham and the Black Country.

Above: *A view of the Oxford Canal at Banbury. No photograph could better depict the incomparable power of the countryside canal to conjure up peace and contentment, with its tree-fringed towpath and surrounding meadows. Anglers sit gazing dreamily at their floats from the rotting hulk 'Doris'.*

Above: Cropredy, Oxford Canal c1960 (C291006).

THE OXFORD CANAL

From Hawkesbury Junction near Coventry to the River Thames at Oxford, and junctions with the Grand Union Canal at Napton and Braunston

The Oxford Canal was first opened as far as Banbury in 1778. Passing through much remote and beautiful countryside, it is a classic example of contour cutting by the engineer Samuel Simcock. There are no locks because the canal hugs the contours of the land with much twisting and wriggling. The penny-conscious owner, Earl Spencer, was highly satisfied, relieved that 'the navigators will have no business to stop for any purpose'. In 1790 it was extended to Oxford, and the city bells were rung to celebrate the arrival of the first barges loaded with coal from Coventry.

Above: The Lock at Cropredy, Oxford Canal c1960 (C291015)

Above: Batchwork Locks, Rickmansworth, Grand Union Canal 1897 (39696)
Below: The Bascule Lift Bridge, Batchworth, Grand Union Canal 1897 (39695)

THE GRAND UNION CANAL

From the Thames at Brentford, Middlesex to Birmingham

The Grand Union was created in the 1920s from a network of independent canals linking London with the industrial towns of the West and East Midlands. The Main Line runs for 137 miles and incorporates 166 locks. At Batchworth, close by Rickmansworth ('Ricky' to the bargemen), there is a fine example of a wide-beamed 'bascule' lift bridge.

Above: Aylesbury, Grand Union Canal 1921 (70564)

Above: The Three Locks, Leighton Buzzard, Grand Union Canal c1955 (L211054) *Previous pages:* Iron Bridge Lock, Watford, Grand Union Canal 1921 (70492)

THE GRAND UNION CANAL

From the Thames at Brentford, Middlesex to Birmingham

In the superb picture of Iron Bridge Lock, Watford (on pages 42 and 43), the horse on the left is waiting to haul George Garside's two barges, which are 'breasted up' together in the lock. The lower regions of the Grand Union were built especially wide to accommodate two boats. The Aylesbury arm of the Grand Union departs from the main line at Marsworth, and has some 16 locks in 6 miles, very narrow and not for the faint-hearted. In the background of the Aylesbury scene shown here, two barges lie moored in a peaceful stretch. Their side cloths are 'sheeted up'. The bargewomen have hung some washing out by the towpath. In the picture on the left, two British Waterways narrow boats are negotiating the Three Locks at Soulbury near Leighton Buzzard. At Blisworth, shown here, is the renowned 3,000 yard tunnel, opened in 1805. It is said the silence inside is 'appalling' and 'deathly still'. A barge is chugging its way past the village. The Grand Union Canal Co. had strategic warehouses here.

Top: Soulbury, Grand Union Canal c1955 (L211049). *Centre:* Blisworth, Grand Union Canal c1955 (B283391)
Above: Tunnel, Daventry, Grand Union Canal c1965 (D83014)

Above: Daventry, Grand Union Canal c1965 (D83042)

THE GRAND UNION CANAL

From the Thames at Brentford, Middlesex to Birmingham

At Braunston the canal drops sharply through six locks. The Grand Junction Canal, now part of the Grand Union, was built in the late 18th century from Braunston to London. With its wide 14 foot locks it offered a quicker route than the winding Oxford Canal and grew rapidly in popularity with barge owners. The village has strong ties for canal people, and many are buried in the cemetry of All Saints Church. In the view of Daventry a motorised narrow boat tows its 'butty' along behind. On the open canal the 'snubber' or towing rope was normally 60 feet long.

Above: Braunston, Grand Union Canal c1965 (B778014)

Above: Kinver, Staffordshire and Worcestershire Canal c1955 (K37080)

THE STAFFORDSHIRE AND WORCESTERSHIRE CANAL

From the River Severn, Stourport to the Trent & Mersey Canal, near Stafford

James Brindley created this successful canal in 1772. It was a vital part of the Grand Cross network that linked the rivers Trent, Severn, Thames and Mersey. Though it passes through an industrial landscape there are many quiet rural stretches where the narrow boats chug along under a dense canopy of green. Unlike many of its rivals, the Staffordshire & Worcestershire never sold out to the railway companies, some of whom made a policy of buying up canals, then running them down so that they could gradually take over their freight business. At Kinver, pictured here, a lofty wooded red sandstone ridge offers delightful views over the Staffordshire countryside. The boy on the right waits with his lock key while the level rises.

Above: Whittington lock, Kinver, Staffs and Worcestershire Canal c1965 (K37144)

THE COVENTRY CANAL

From Coventry to Fradley near Lichfield, Staffordshire

Created in 1790, this successful canal was built to ship Bedworth coals to the town of Coventry. At Hopwas, just beyond Tamworth, the canal threads its way through attractive wooded country.

THE BIRMINGHAM CANAL NAVIGATIONS

Canals serving Birmingham and the Black Country

On the previous pages is a superb view of a breasted-up pair of narrow boats owned by Thomas Clayton of Oldbury. They specialised in carrying waste products of the gas industry. Note the bargewoman in traditional long dress, pinafore and white head shawl. The horse on the right is being led along the towpath to be hitched up.

Above: Hopwas, Coventry Canal c1955 (H413001)

Above: Hopwas, Coventry Canal c1955 (H413002) *Previous pages:* Near Oldbury, Birmingham Canal Navigations c1920 (O128501)

Above: The Lock House, Colwich, Trent and Mersey Canal c1955 (C565005)

THE NORTH MIDLANDS

The canal network of this region connects the industrial towns of the Birmingham Canal Navigations with the great port of Liverpool and the Mersey, and with the northern cities of Lancashire and Yorkshire. The Trent & Mersey links the famous Bridgewater Canal at Manchester with the River Trent Navigation of the North East. The Shropshire Union journeys from Wolverhampton to join with the Manchester Ship Canal at Ellesmere Port. It also has connections with the Llangollen Canal, the exquisite waterway that features the grandiose aqueduct at Pontcysyllte. The River Dee is an ancient navigation flowing through Chester and under the Pontcysyllte Aqueduct. It reaches the North Wales coast at Point of Air. The Macclesfield Canal provides a vital link between the Trent & Mersey, the Peak Forest Canal and the mill towns of West Yorkshire.

Above: *This view shows the attractive lock keeper's cottage and stone bridge at Colwich. Part of the great charm of Britain's canal system is in the simple, homely quality of its architecture.*

Above: Great Haywood, Trent and Mersey Canal c1955 (G303010)

Above: Great Haywood, Trent and Mersey Canal c1955 (G303011)

Above: Brewood, Shropshire Union Canal c1965 (B68003)

THE TRENT AND MERSEY CANAL

From the Bridgewater Canal at Preston Brook to the Trent at Shardlow, Derbyshire

At Great Haywood Junction the Trent & Mersey meets with the Staffordshire & Worcestershire Canal. Clay was shipped along this canal to Wedgwood's potteries, and on the return trip the barges provided slow and sure distribution for the fragile china.

THE SHROPSHIRE UNION CANAL

From the Staffordshire & Worcestershire Canal near Wolverhampton to Ellesmere Port, Cheshire

The Shropshire Union Canal is an amalgamation of the Chester, Ellesmere, Birmingham and Liverpool Junction. It was the main railway-owned canal (the LMS) and was formed in 1864. It ran successfully until the Second World War, and in its hey-day operated almost 700 craft of various kinds.
At Brewood, pronounced 'Brood', the canal threads its way through a narrow rocky cutting. Here we see a row of moored craft converted to houseboats.

THE SHROPSHIRE UNION CANAL

From the Staffordshire & Worcestershire Canal near Wolverhampton to Ellesmere Port, Cheshire

Throughout a long stretch of over twenty miles the canal maintains a level until it reaches Wheaton Aston, pictured here. The narrow boat in the view below has just emerged from Tyrley Locks near Market Drayton. It has been converted to a tanker, with characteristic flat decking, and was probably carrying bulk liquids. The five locks at Tyrley negotiate a fall of over thirty feet. Opposite is a classic scene of a narrow boat close by the Tyrley locks in the early years of this century. It is probably a 'Number One', the owner having just a single horse and his own boat. The horse is deep in his nosebag, enjoying a feed after the long haul through the lock. Life was hard and rough and ready for the one-man operation. Bargemen worked 6 or 7 day weeks, received no sick pay and no salary during freeze-ups. Yet they doubtless relished their independence and enjoyed the beautiful scenery. Most kept to steady routes and sought regular contract business.

Top: The Lock, Wheaton Aston, Shropshire Union Canal c1955 (W286009). *Centre:* Canal Bridge, Market Drayton, Shropshire Union Canal c1955 (M32031R) *Above:* Tyrley Locks, Market Drayton, Shropshire Union Canal c1955 (M32035) *Opposite:* Tyrley Locks 1911 (63346)

Above: View of the Aqueduct and Viaduct, Chirk, Llangollen Canal c1955 (C366039)
Below: The Aqueduct and Railway Viaduct, Chirk, Llangollen Canal c1955(L366022)

THE LLANGOLLEN CANAL

From the Shropshire Union near Nantwich, Cheshire to Llangollen, Clwyd

Constructed by Telford and Jessop to link the rivers Severn, Dee and Mersey, the Llangollen Canal is one of the most popular waterways in the country. A little beyond the 450 yard long tunnel at Chirk, the canal is suddenly carried 70 feet in the air over a spectacular stone aqueduct. Hugging it closely all the way is the railway vidauct.

Above: The Ferry over the River Dee, Eccleston 1895 (36455)

THE RIVER DEE

From Farndon near Wrexham, Clwyd to Point of Air on the North Wales Coast

The River Dee rises at Bala, and makes an 80 mile dash for the sea, sweeping through a dangerous switchback of rapids and rocks to Llangollen. Here it dips under Telford's masterpiece, the magnificent Pontcysyllte Aqueduct on the Welsh section of the Shropshire Union Canal. At Eccleston, just up river from Chester, it charts a more leisurely course. Here we see holiday makers being carried across the Dee on the chain ferry. In the picture below, a steam launch is approaching the jetty.

Above: The Ferry over the Dee, Eccleston c1886 (1722)

THE RIVER DEE

From Farndon near Wrexham, Clwyd to Point of Air on the North Wales Coast

The river at Chester bustles with pleasure craft. The town sits on a sandstone spur north of the Dee, which winds past the ancient castle, begun in 1069, but now much modified by late 18th-century additions. The pictures below and opposite show the delicate and beautiful suspension footbridge. A steam launch is passing underneath. Below the weir at Chester, the Dee was a busy commercial waterway until silting up prevented seagoing vessels from reaching the city. Above the weir was a boating playground.

Above: The River Dee at Chester 1923 (73882)

Above: The Suspension Bridge over the Dee, Chester 1914 (67546)

Above: The Groves, River Dee, Chester 1923 (73875)

THE MACCLESFIELD CANAL

From Marple Junction on the Peak Forest Canal, Cheshire to Hall Green on the Trent & Mersey Canal

This canal had a late start and only opened in 1831. By then the railways had already forced many canals into steep decline. Yet the Macclesfield Canal prospered against all odds, offering a short, direct passage from the North Midlands to Manchester. It was laid out by Telford, who showed his characteristic genius for finding the simplest and most even contour levels. He managed to restrict locks to a single flight at Bosley. Today the Macclesfield threads its way through remote, picturesque country. The picture below shows a peaceful scene a little beyond the Bosley locks near Congleton. Between steep wooded slopes the canal winds under the tiny stone Dane Valley bridge. Farmworkers stand and stare. At Congleton the canal crosses the River Dane over an aqueduct.

Above: The Macclesfield Canal, Congleton 1898 (42175)

Above: George's Dock, Liverpool c1881 (14149)

AROUND MERSEYSIDE

The Mersey is the vital lifeline for northern industry, and almost all of the canals and navigations in the region head towards it or have links with it. Merseyside is the home of some of England's busiest and most impressive inland waterways. The River Weaver creates a link with the Trent & Mersey Canal by way of the mighty Anderton vertical lift. An impressive modern commercial waterway, it acts as a funnel for industrial products from Cheshire, carrying them down to Weston Point Docks, where there is a link with the Manchester Ship Canal. The Bridgewater Canal was the pioneering scheme that precipitated the great canal building era. It was built to link the Duke of Bridgewater's coal mines with the city of Manchester. A triumph of engineering, it features the famous Barton Aqueduct. At Runcorn there was once a flight of locks connecting the Bridgewater with the Manchester Ship Canal, the magnificent seaway that opened in 1894, and which brought the city of Manchester the vital link it had wanted with the Mersey at Eastham.

Above: *The great port of Liverpool has been a lifeline for sea-going freight in Britain for centuries. The docks stretch for 7 miles.*

Above: The Swing Bridge over the River Weaver, Northwich 1900 (45421)

Above: The Swing Bridge over the River Weaver, Northwich 1900 (45422)

THE RIVER WEAVER

From Winsford Bridge, Cheshire to Weston Point Docks, and junction with Manchester Ship Canal

In the 18th century, sailing barges called at Winsford from the Mersey carrying salt from the great mines of Cheshire. Since those early days, the Weaver has undergone a massive improvement programme, making it one of the most efficient commercial waterways in Britain. The Anderton Boat Lift connects the river with the Trent and Mersey Canal. A pair of narrow boats could be lifted 50 feet in two caissons. The Anderton Lift created a much faster passage for boats and increased the tonnage of river traffic to 226,000 in 1913. It was converted to electric power in 1906 and extensively renovated in 1974.

Above: Hunts Lock, Northwich c1960 (N43024)

Above: The Anderton Boat Lift, Northwich c1960 (N43026)

Above: The Locks, Runcorn, Bridgewater Canal c1955 (R67003)

THE BRIDGEWATER CANAL

From Castleford Junction with the Rochdale Canal, Manchester to Runcorn, Cheshire

The Duke of Bridgewater has been called the 'the parent and father' of our canal system. In 1760 he employed the pioneering engineer, James Brindley, to create a waterway connecting his coal mines with the growing city of Manchester. Brindley enjoyed a reputation for 'handling rocks as easily as you would plum pies'. It was said that visitors swooned when they saw the famous Barton aqueduct, which was demolished in the 1890s. At Runcorn there was once a huge flight of locks connecting the Bridgewater with the Manchester Ship Canal. They were designed to admit the small sailing barges called 'flats' that worked the Mersey. Over the page, a motorised Fellows, Morton & Clayton narrow boat awaits its turn. It has the characteristic Z-shaped metal rudder head.

Above: The Docks, Runcorn c1900 (R67301)

Above: The Transporter Bridge, Runcorn 1899 (43432A)

Above: Near the Locks at Runcorn, Bridgewater Canal c1955 (R67002)

Above: The Bridgewater Canal at Lymm c1960 (L122054)
Below: The Bridgewater Canal at Lymm c1960 (L122026)

THE BRIDGEWATER CANAL

From Castleford Junction with the Rochdale Canal, Manchester to Runcorn, Cheshire

In the view of Lymm at the top of the page, two of Horsfield's craft are hauling coal, the once horse-drawn butty being towed by the motorised narrow boat. The picture below shows the Clio gliding under the bridge of this pleasant little town, with its cluster of canal-side cottages. On the right, in front of the bridge, is a lifting winch.

Above: The Swing Bridge, Warrington, Manchester Ship Canal c1960 (W29056)

Above: The Manchester Ship Canal 1894 (33810)

THE MANCHESTER SHIP CANAL

From the River Mersey at Easton to Manchester

The city of Manchester was the powerhouse of northern industry. The fact that all of its manufacturing products had to be shipped through the port of Liverpool - its arch-rival - dented the city fathers' pride. They demanded an outlet to the sea, and got one in 1894 at a cost of over £14,000,000. It was a masterpiece of automated engineering. 200 huge steam excavators mounted on rails hauled up ton after ton of spoil into 6,000 wagons. 16,000 workers laboured for seven years before it was finished. This superb new seaway, with its deep-water berths, brought Manchester a huge trading advantage. One impressive feature was the new Barton Aqueduct, designed by Edward Leader Williams. It carried the Bridgewater Canal across the new waterway. It pivoted on a central support.

Above: Barton Swing Aqueduct, Manchester Ship Canal 1895 (33693)

Above: Latchford Locks, Manchester Ship Canal 1895 (33697) *Overleaf:* Barton Bridge, Manchester Ship Canal 1895 (33691)

Above: The Chelmer and Blackwater Navigation, Maldon 1906 (55547)

EAST ANGLIA AND THE FENS

Suffolk has several important rivers and navigations along its coastal fringes. On the Chelmer & Blackwater Navigation barges carried timber and coals to the town of Chelmsford. Ipswich and Felixstowe are served by the River Orwell. A major network is centred on the Great Ouse, one of England's greatest rivers, which links Bedford with the Wash near King's Lynn. It has important junctions with the Middle Level Navigation of the Fens, and with the picturesque River Cam that runs through Cambridge. The River Witham links Lincoln with the Wash. The Norfolk Broads are a pleasure seeker's delight, with mile upon mile of open water, connected by the rivers Bure, Yare, Thurne and Waveney.

Above: *A plodding horse hauls a shallow-draught barge carrying a load of lime. This waterway was one of the last to be dug, and had a short commercial life because of successful poaching by the railways. At Heybridge Basin, near Maldon, huge colliery barges offloaded their coal for onward delivery to the town of Chelmsford. Many returned loaded with timber or manure.*

Above: The River Colne, Colchester 1895 (35506)

THE RIVER COLNE

From Colne Point, on the Essex coast, to Colchester

This old waterway has been in use for centuries, and allowed small coasters to travel up to the port of Colchester. Today it is a paradise for leisure craft.

THE RIVER ORWELL

From Ipswich, Suffolk to Felixstowe on the coast

Ipswich has age-old seafaring associations. Defoe records that he saw 'perhaps two hundred sail of ships' lying by the town during the winter months, 'as safe as in a wet dock'. For centuries cloth was exported to the continent and, later, iron and coal. The waterfront is crowded with huge warehouses and granaries. The picture here shows barges clamouring at the lock gates.

Above: The Lock Gates, The River Orwell, Ipswich 1921 (70413)

Above: St Peter's Dock, Ipswich, River Orwell 1921 (70411)

THE RIVER ORWELL

From Ipswich, Suffolk to Felixstowe on the coast

The River Orwell is Suffolk's most navigable waterway. Ships can enter or leave whatever the state of the tide. Ipswich's Wet Dock was built in the early 1840s and was then the finest and largest in the country. Great sailing ships waited down river to tranship their cargoes into sailing barges before heading up into the Wet Dock. The quay was lined with great mills like those shown in the picture here. Some, like Cranfields and Pauls, owned their own fleets of sailing barges. These flat, shallow-draught craft could carry an awesome cargo. The one shown here is loaded to sinking point with heavy sacks. Ipswich attracted a huge amount of heavy industry, too, with companies in the town manufacturing boilers, cranes, lawnmowers and agricultural machinery.

Above: Holywell Ferry, St Ives, The Great Ouse 1914 (66972)
Below: The Old River, St Ives 1914 (66958)

THE GREAT OUSE

From Bedford to the Wash, near King's Lynn, Norfolk

In the 17th century, the ingenious Dutch engineer Cornelius Vermuyden forged a navigation from the sea cross-country to the town of Bedford. Much of the land through which the Ouse idles has dropped fifteen feet in level since, and is now highly fertile farmland. The thatched Ferry Boat Inn, at Holywell, St Ives, shown here, has been selling beer to customers since before William the Conqueror.

THE GREAT OUSE

From Bedford to the Wash, near King's Lynn, Norfolk

The silt of centuries has robbed the town of King's Lynn of much of its former glory. It was once one of Britain's greatest ports, thronged with ships from Germany, Holland and the Baltic. It is now two miles inland. An impressive tideway carries the Ouse into the Wash below the docks, which were built in the Victorian era. Where once mighty ships plied their trade, there are now just a few tiny boats shrimping and collecting mussels. The handsome Custom House was built in 1681 by Henry Bell. With its pyramid roof, gallery and cupola, it retains a quiet dignity in the midst of our brash, modern age.

Above: The Quay, King's Lynn 1898 (40893).

Above: The Customs House, King's Lynn, The Great Ouse 1898 (40878)

Above: On the River Granta, Cambridge 1914 (66906)

THE RIVERS CAM AND GRANTA

The Cam - from a junction with the Great Ouse near Ely, to Cambridge. The Granta - rising near Thaxtead Essex

The River Cam is navigable as far as Cambridge through Jesus Lock, where it provides a tranquil focal point to this graceful university city. A trip through Cambridge on the river is an unforgettable experience. Flowing behind the colleges along the Backs, it bustles with punts and skiffs, against a backdrop of silken college lawns that stretch elegantly down to the waters. The Cam flows through much wide, wind-swept and desolate fen country on its route to Cambridge. Fringed with sedges and reeds, the Fens can have a brooding, bleak atmosphere on a dark winter's day, the winds bitter and keen.

Above: Jesus Lock, The River Cam, Cambridge 1925 (78731B)
Overleaf: The Eights, Cambridge 1909 (61510)

TEAS

THE NORFOLK BROADS

Navigations of the Yare, Bure, Ant, Thurne and Waveney

These shallow lakes have been called the pleasure grounds of Norfolk, and are the remains of a huge estuary that once spread over much of the eastern part of the county. No one is completely certain as to their origin, but it is believed they are the result of medieval peat workings. At Acle, on the River Bure, wherries and sailing craft glide by under the old bridge, their masts lowered. The Fens have been likened to a crust of bread floating on a bowl of water, and it can often be hard to determine where the water ends and the land begins. The vast skies, romantic windmills, piping seabirds and desolate wastes of the Broads are strongly reminiscent of the work of the old Dutch landscape painters.

Above: The River Bure at Acle c1929 (A204048)

Above: Entrance to the River Thurne, Acle c1926 (A204049)

Above: Ranworth Broad c1960 (R9047)

THE NORFOLK BROADS

Navigations of the Yare, Bure, Ant, Thurne and Waveney

In the picture of Ranworth shown here, reed for thatching has been offloaded onto the bank. It is cut in the winter when the long leaves have been stripped by frost. Reeds are cropped each year, regular harvesting ensuring straight, clean growth. The Broad comes right up to the edge of the village, its 90 acres of open water surrounded by picturesque woodland and marsh, the haunt of wild birds. Horning is a popular focus of Broadland, with yachts and wherries clogging the waterway alongside the ferry. The Norfolk Wherry, shown overleaf, was designed to sail exceptionally close to the wind, as tacking can be a hazardous if not impossible job in these narrow waterways. Averaging 60 feet long, the wherries have a massive high-peaked mainsail.

Above: The Ferry, Horning, River Bure 1921 (70902)

Above: Near Horning, River Bure 1902 (48108)

Above: The Old Mill, Horstead, near Coltishall, River Bure 1902 (48149)

THE NORFOLK BROADS

Navigations of the Yare, Bure, Ant, Thurne and Waveney

The old mill at Horstead near Coltishall on the River Bure, shown opposite, would have seen many wherries drawn up at its wharf. Coltishall is the gateway to the Broads, set on a low hill above the winding Bure. The old lock has long been derelict, and pleasure craft now moor by the riverside, which is set apart from the cottages and village street by meadows. When the throngs of summer visitors, yachts, launches and cruisers disappear with the swallows, the Broads sink back into their true nature, timeless and brooding. The picture of the solitary old woman in bonnet and pinafore dress, pushing off from the bank across the dark waters, with menacing clouds overhead, encapsulates their unique and peculiar atmosphere.

Top: The Lock, Coltishall, River Bure c1955 (C417037). *Centre:* The Staithe, Coltishall, River Bure c1955 (C417070)
Above: The Evening Ferry c1900 (T213073)

THE MIDDLE LEVEL NAVIGATIONS

A complex of navigable drainage channels linking the River Nene near Peterborough with the tidal Ouse.

The five mile-long Wisbech Canal once connected the villages of Outwell and Upwell with the River Nene at Wisbech. It has since been filled in and closed down. Wisbech is the capital of the Fens. It was once a strategic sea port, where coasters transhipped their cargoes into fenland lighters. Yet the tides have played the town foul over the centuries, silting up successive estuaries of the River Nene so that now the town is stranded ten miles from the sea. Yet ships still struggle their way in to berth at the quaysides of the town. At low tide they are knee deep in mud. In the view of the canal at Wisbech opposite, the old lock is in the background.

Above: Upwell, Middle Level Navigations 1923 (73591).

Above: Wisbech, Middle Level Navigations 1901 (47584) *Opposite:* The Canal, Wisbech 1929 (81972)

Above: The River Witham at Lincoln 1890 (25620)
Below: The River Witham at Boston 1890 (26067)

THE RIVER WITHAM

From the Fossdyke Canal at Lincoln to the Wash

This ancient waterway, once bustling with commercial craft, is now the haunt of yachts and launches. At Lincoln, warehouses cluster at the water's edge. Boston lies in tidal waters beyond the 18th-century Great Sluice, which was built to control flooding. Fine old sailing ships, like the one shown here, once thronged the quayside. The Mayflower set sail from Boston in 1620, taking the Pilgrim Fathers to America.

Above: The Docks, Boston 1890 (26082)

Above: Stamford on the River Welland, from the Meadows 1922 (72296)

Above: Trent Bridge, Nottingham, River Trent 1902 (48328)

THE NORTH AND NORTH EAST

This is a region rich in great rivers and canals. The River Trent joins the industrial Midlands, by way of the Trent & Mersey Canal, to the Yorkshire Ouse and Humber. It also has a junction with the Sheffield & South Yorkshire Navigation, which serves the bustling factory towns of Yorkshire. The Leeds & Liverpool Canal was the greatest of the trans-Pennine waterways, connecting the Aire & Calder Navigation at Leeds with the port of Liverpool. One important branch connects Wigan with the Bridgewater Canal at Leigh. With its wide-beam locks that accommodated the famous 'short' boats, it formed a strategic link between the rivers of the east - the Don, Wharfe, Derwent and Trent - and the industrial cities of Lancashire. The Leeds & Liverpool boasts the impressive flight of staircase locks at Bingley.

Above: *Still a formidable waterway, with much commercial traffic journeying to Nottingham, the Trent was once busy with steam tugs and Humber keel sailing barges.*

THE RIVER TRENT

From Shardlow near junction with the Trent & Mersey to Trent Falls, junction with Rivers Humber and Ouse

The River Trent is navigable for some 93 miles, and plays a vital role in linking the waterways of the North East with those of the Midlands. Before 1900, goods were transhipped to smaller boats at Newark. The river was only navigable from Trent Falls as far as the town. Beyond Newark it entered a fast-flowing and shallow stretch that was impassable for larger vessels bound for Nottingham. By the end of the Great War the river floor was dredged to a minimum depth of five feet and several locks were added. Nottingham was now less than a day's journey away from the port of Hull, which greatly increased its prosperity.

Above: Town Lock, Newark, River Trent c1965 (N12107)

Above: View on the River Trent, Newark 1906 (56505).

Above: Doncaster, Sheffield & S Yorks Navigation 1903 (49857)

THE SHEFFIELD AND SOUTH YORKSHIRE NAVIGATION

From the River Trent at Keadby, Lincolnshire, to Sheffield, Yorkshire

With its 29 automated locks, this modern, commercial waterway has a link with sea-going ships at the port of Goole. The S & SY was established in 1895, and was created from a grouping of several much older waterways, including the Stainforth & Keady and Sheffield Canals. In the view of Sheffield here, the canal basin is thronged with Yorkshire keels loaded heavily with coals and metal. They were sturdily built with oak planks up to 3" thick. Coals and industrial products from the Don valley have helped create prosperity in Sheffield and Doncaster and ensured a flourishing river life.

Above: The Canal Basin, Sheffield, Sheffield and S Yorkshire Navigation c1870 (S108001)

Above: Sprotbrough, River Don, 1895 (35327)

THE RIVER DON

From Dunford Bridge, S Yorkshire, via Rotherham and Doncaster, to Goole, Humberside

At Sprotbrough, close by Doncaster, the River Don flows between heavily wooded banks. There are two fine old bridges and a weir. The architecture of the bridges, locks and cottages respond closely to the geology of the area. Usually, local materials are used, so that the canals harmonise perfectly with their surroundings. The Don is liable to flooding, and engineers have installed flood locks that can be operated if a spate is about to occur.

Above: Sprotbrough, River Don 1895 (35328)

Above: The River Aire, Bingley 1923 (74415)
Below: River Aire and Weir, Bingley 1923 (74412)

THE RIVER AIRE

From Malham via Skipton, Bingley and Leeds, Yorkshire to join the Ouse above Boothferry Bridge, Humberside

The River Aire cuts a winding course through broad pastures, stony valleys and bustling industrial areas, on its way to join the Ouse and the open sea at Asselby Island. It joins the important Aire and Calder Navigation at Knottingley, where the waterway twists and turns for six miles. At Bingley mills crowd down to the waterside. It also accompanies the Leeds & Liverpool Canal at Kirkstall.

Above: Bingley, Five Rise Locks 1894 (34748)
Overleaf: Bingley, Five Rise Locks c1900 (B98501)

THE LEEDS AND LIVERPOOL CANAL

From the Aire & Calder Navigation at Leeds to Liverpool and the River Mersey

At 127 miles, this is the longest canal in Britain, and creates a vital trans-Pennine crossing between the mill towns of Yorkshire and the sea ports of the Mersey. It was designed to be a broad canal, with locks that could handle barges up to 14 feet wide - the regular narrow boats had a width of just 7 feet. The scenery is magnificent, the canal threading a path through open moorland, past the atmospheric ruins of Kirkstall Abbey, and between dark, overhanging woods. Below the famous Five-Rise staircase locks at Bingley, boatmen can see the towers and factories of Titus Salt's pioneering industrial village, Saltaire. Raising barges and boats through an awesome 60 feet lift, these locks are not for the beginner: operating the paddles in the wrong way can cause a tidal wave! Over the page, a transom-sterned 'short boat', loaded with coal, waits to enter the flight. It is being towed by a steam tug, but would have originally been pulled by horses. With its sweeping lines and long wooden tiller, it could carry a load twice the size of a narrow boat.

709
LEEDS

Robert
J.R. THORNTON
709
LEEDS

THE LEEDS AND LIVERPOOL CANAL

From the Aire & Calder Navigation at Leeds, Yorkshire to Liverpool and the River Mersey

Work on the Leeds & Liverpool began in 1770. Not only did the coming of the canal vastly lower distribution costs for the industrial towns of Yorkshire, it also provided a localised transport service for the towns and cities through which it passed. Skipton was linked up in 1773 as part of the relatively simple first section, which needed no locks. The sections from Leeds to Gargrave and Wigan to Liverpool followed by 1777. Then the funding ran out. For years progress was slow, but the missing stages were finally completed in 1816.

Above: Leeds and Liverpool Canal, Skipton Woods c1960 (S137026)

Above: Boating at Skipton, Leeds and Liverpool Canal 1911 (63581)

Above: The River Wharfe at Tadcaster 1906 (54849)

THE RIVER WHARFE

From the Yorkshire Ouse above Cawood to Tadcaster, Yorkshire

Barges plied up and down the Wharfe delivering to the breweries, including John Smith's at Tadcaster, pictured here. It was prone to flooding, and the Victorians were forced to move a church further up the bank out of reach of the invading waters. Here, a long, rickety and precarious plank stretches from the moored sailing barge in the centre of the river to the bank.

THE RIVER NIDD

From Great Whernside, Yorkshire, via Knaresborough to join the Yorkshire Ouse at Nun Monkton

Impassable to commercial river traffic, the Nidd drops swiftly from the Pennines down to Knaresborough, where rapids wait in ambush for the unwary punter paddling furiously through dark, romantic gorges.

Above: The Rapids over the River Nidd, Knaresborough 1914 (67266)

THE RIVER NIDD

From Great Whernside, Yorkshire, via Knaresborough to join the Yorkshire Ouse at Nun Monkton

At Knaresborough the river scenery is magnificent. The water glides under the grandiose railway viaduct with its lofty arches and embattled parapet. The picturesque gardens of the hillside houses rise in tiers over the rocky cliffs, and flights of steps climb up into the streets of the town from the river below. Punts and skiffs idle in the water. There was once a thriving linen trade here, and the bolts of cloth were shipped out through the tiny port of Boroughbridge.

Above: The River Nidd at Knaresborough 1911 (63532)

Above: The River Nidd at Knaresborough 1921 (71673)

THE YORKSHIRE OUSE

From Ouse Gill Beck, Yorkshire, via York to Trent Falls, the junction of the Rivers Humber and Trent

Barges ply the river as far upstream as York but no further. The upper picture of the canal basin shows clinker-built sloops unloading at the wharfside. The wooden covers have been lifted off. In the late 1800s, the clinker construction method of overlapping planks gave way to the more efficient smooth-sided carvel system. Across the canal, nestling under the old city walls, are the ramshackle premises of a wholesale coal merchant.

THE RIVERS HULL AND HUMBER

R Hull - from Struncheon Hill Lock to Hull
R Humber - from Trent Falls and the River Trent to Hull and Grimsby, Humberside

The waters of four rivers flow past the Alexandra Docks at Hull, pictured here - the Yorkshire Ouse, Trent, Hull and Humber. In this busy scene, a ship is offloading its cargo into barges.

THE RIPON CANAL

From the River Ure at Oxclose Lock to Ripon, Yorkshire

Ripon is the farthest north a barge can travel without being removed from the water. This short, 2 mile canal was opened in 1773, and is an extension of the River Ure. In the view of the stone-walled canal basin on this page we see the Minster rising over the roofs, and the old arched bridge.

Above: Alexandra Docks, Hull 1903 (49825)

Above: The Ripon Canal at Ripon c1885 (18318) *Opposite:* The River Wear at Durham 1892 (30734)

Above: Derwentwater, The Lake District 1906 (54982)

THE NORTH WEST

The north west is not rich in commercial waterways. The River Ribble flows down from the Yorkshire Dales towards Preston, once a major cotton town, where great ships moored at the dock. The Lancaster Canal begins its course at Ashton Basin at Preston, heading for Carnforth. It has a complex history, and was originally built at the request of the merchants of Lancaster, who were keen to have a distribution link with the Bridgewater Canal near Liverpool. What remains of the Lancaster is just a fragment of the original system, and isolated from the rest of the national network. The Lake District is a uniquely magnificent region of lakes set amidst mountains. Boats cluster around the port of Bowness on Lake Windermere, and in summer the waters are thronged with pleasure cruisers and steamers.

Above: *The River Derwent flows out of Derwentwater into Bassenthwaite. The two lakes were once a single stretch of water, but the streams flowing towards each other deposited silt, forming a land barrier between. The picture here shows Friars Crag and Causey Pike.*

Above: The Bowness Ferry Boat, The Lake District 1896 (38800)

Above: The Boat Station, Bowness, The Lake District 1896 (38791)

Above: Coniston, Waterhead, The Lake District 1912 (64281)
Below: Yachts on Windermere, The Lake District 1896 (38804)

THE LAKE DISTRICT

Coniston Water

With is glorious setting of fells and woods, Coniston Water has long been popular with trippers. Pleasure steamers set out on the water at Lakebank at the southern end, filled to bursting, and passengers enjoyed the delights of this beautiful 5 mile long stretch of inland water. The view above shows what is probably the luxurious steamboat, Gondola, which was built in 1859.

THE LAKE DISTRICT

Bowness on Windermere

The picture on page 102 shows the Bowness ferry in 1896. A coach and four carries a party of well-heeled passengers across Lake Windermere. The horses are steadied by the ferryman - a sudden burst of steam from the ferry engine might startle them. Overleaf is another beautiful photograph of the ferry setting out across the broad, placid waters. A woman is fishing from the bank.

Above: Bowness, Windermere, The Lake District 1929 (82809)

Above: The Ferry Boat, Windermere, The Lake District 1887 (20462) *Overleaf:* The Ferry Boat, Bowness, The Lake District 1896 (38802)

Above: Windermere and Miller Ground 1926 (79185)

Above: Bowness Pier, Windermere, The Lake District 1887 (20451)

THE LAKE DISTRICT

Windermere

Windermere is the greatest of England's lakes. Ten miles long, it has a bewildering number of islands, creeks, bays and wooded shores. The first passenger steamers were introduced in 1845, plying to and from the tiny port of Bowness. The romantic setting of the lake and the mountains around it were particularly appealing to the Victorians, who had been brought up to appreciate majestic scenery. A few miles away at Grasmere, the great poet of wild places, William Wordsworth, had raged passionately at the growing numbers of visitors, as well as the rash of new retirement homes and villas that were springing up all over his beloved hills. It seems the Lakes were overrun even in the 19th century.

Above: The Docks, Preston, River Ribble 1893 (33097)
Below: The River Ribble at Preston 1903 (50077)

THE RIVER RIBBLE

From Gayle Moor, N Yorkshire, via Settle and Preston to the sea near Southport

Spilling down from the Yorkshire Dales, the Ribble streams under the lovely old bridge at Settle, through the valley that has taken its name. It skirts Clitheroe then snakes its way towards the busy industrial town of Preston. Here, great ships inch their way up to the docks through the sandbanks by Lytham St Anne's. Preston was a major cotton town, and the Lancaster Canal runs from Ashton Basin.

THE LANCASTER CANAL

From Ashton Basin, Preston via Garstang to Tewitfield Locks, Carnforth, Lancashire

This beautiful canal, with its magnificent sea views of Morecambe Bay, was originally the vision of the factory owners of Lancaster who were keen to connect their mills with the national canal network via the Bridgewater. Stone, slate and lime would be carried from the north and Wigan coal from the south. By 1819 the designer John Rennie had constructed a canal from Kendal in the north down to Wigan, remarkable for the ingenuity of its design. Yet the Ribble near Preston was never bridged by Rennie's planned aqueduct and there was just a temporary plate tramway. Lancaster's dream was never fulfilled. Much of the canal's course in the north is now derelict.

Above: Six Arches Bridge, River Calder, by Lancaster Canal c1960 (G238063)

Above: The Wharf, Garstang, Lancaster Canal c1955 (G238013)

Above: The Lancaster Canal, near Lancaster 1896 (37384)
Below: Broken Bridge, Lancaster, Lancaster Canal 1918 (68332)
Overleaf: The Lancaster Canal at Carnforth 1918 (68306)

THE LANCASTER CANAL

From Ashton Basin, Preston via Garstang to Tewitfield Locks, Carnforth, Lancashire

Broken Back Bridge at Lancaster, shown here, has peculiar stonework, which dips and tumbles out of true. The bridge arch is picked out in white paint so that bargemen could see the opening when they passed through at late evening. Over the page, the broad-beamed vessel loaded with hay is hauled by two horses, feeding as they wait for the photographer.

INDEX

Abingdon, 24
Acle, 78
Aire, River, 90
Avon, River, Bristol, 15-17
Avon, River, Warwickshire, 37-38
Ayelsbury, 44
Aylesford, 7
Banbury, 39
Barton, 67, 68-69
Basingstoke Canal, 26
Bath, 31
Bathampton, 31
Bingley, 90, 91, 92-93
Birmingham Canal Navigations, 48-49
Blisworth, 45
Boston, 84, 85
Bowness, 101, 103, 104-105
Braunton, 46
Brewood, 53
Bridgewater Canal, 63-65
Bristol, 15, 16-17
Bude, 14
Bude Canal 14
Cam, River, 75-77
Cambridge, 75, 76-77
Carnforth, 110-111
Caversham 22
Chalford, 34
Chelmer and Blackwater Navigation, 70
Cherwell, River, 32
Chester, 58, 59
Chichester, 9
Chichester Canal, 9
Chirk, 56
Colchester, 71
Colne, River, 71
Coltishall, 81
Colwich, 51
Congleton. 59
Coniston, 102
Coventry Canal, 50
Cropredy, 40
Daventry, 45, 46
Dee, River, 57-59
Derwentwater, 100
Devizes, 30
Don, River, 89
Doncaster, 88
Durham, 99
Eccleston, 57
Evesham, 37
Exeter, 10, 11, 12
Exeter Ship Canal, 10-12
Fowey, River, 13
Fowey, 13
Frimley Green, 26
Garstang, 108
Gloucester, 35
Godalming, 28
Goring, 23
Grand Union Canal, 41-46
Granta, River, 76-77
Great Haywood, 52
Great Ouse, River, 73-74
Guildford, 28
Henley, 21
Hertford, 25
Holt Fleet, 36
Hopwas, 50
Horning, 79, 80
Horstead, 80
Hull, River, 98
Hull, 98
Humber, River, 98
Hungerford, 29
Iffley, 24
Ipswich, 71, 72
Kennet and Avon Canal, 29-31
King's Lynn, 74
Kingsbridge, 13
Kinver, 47
Knaresborough, 95, 96
Lake District, 100-106
Lancaster, 109
Lancaster Canal, 108-111
Lee, River, 25
Leeds and Liverpool Canal, 91-94
Leighton Buzzard, 44
Lewes, 9
Lincoln, 84
Liverpool, 60
Llangollen Canal, 56
Lydney, 33
Lydney Canal, 33
Lymm, 65
Macclesfield Canal, 59
Maidenhead, 20
Maidstone, 8
Maldon, 70
Manchester Ship Canal, 66-69
Mapledurham, 23
Market Drayton, 54, 55
Medway Navigation, 7-8
Middle Level Navigations, 82-83
Molesey, 19, 20
Newark, 87
Nidd, River, 95-96
Norfolk Broads, 78-81
Northwich, 61, 62
Nottingham, 86
Odiham, 26
Oldbury, 48-49
Orwell, River, 71-72
Ouse, River, Sussex, 9
Oxford, 32
Oxford Canal, 39-40
Preston, 107
Ranworth, 79
Ranworth Broad, 79
Reading, 22
Ribble, River, 107
Rickmansworth, 41
Ripon, 98
Ripon Canal, 98
Rother, River, 8
Runcorn, 63, 64
Rye, 8
Salcombe, River, 12
Send, 27
Severn, River, 35-37
Sheffield, 88
Sheffield and S Yorkshire Navigation, 88
Shrewsbury, 36
Shropshire Union Canal, 53-55
Skipton, 94
Sonning, 21
Soulbury, 45
Sprotbrough, 89
St Ives, 73
Staffordshire and Worcs Canal, 47
Stamford, 85
Stourport, 37
Stratford, 38
Streatley, 24
Stroudwater Canal, 34
Tadcaster, 95
Teddington, 18
Tewkesbury, 38
Thames, River, 18-24
Trent, River, 86-87
Trent and Mersey Canal, 51-52
Upwell, 82
Warrington, 66
Watford, 41, 42-43
Wear, River, 99
Weaver, River, 61-62
Welland, River, 85
Wey Navigation, 27-28
Wharfe, River, 95
Wheaton Aston, 54
Windermere, 102, 103, 106
Wisbech, 82, 83
Witham, River, 84-85
Worcester, 36
York, 97
Yorkshire Ouse, 97